For those on the front line. With thanks.

DRAW WITH ROB®

HarperCollins *Children's* Books

First published in paperback in Great Britain by
HarperCollins *Children's Books* in 2020

HarperCollins *Children's Books* is a division of HarperCollins*Publishers* Ltd.
Draw With Rob logo ® Rob Biddulph
Text and illustrations copyright © Rob Biddulph 2020
The author/illustrator asserts the moral right to
be identified as the author/illustrator of the work.
A CIP catalogue record for this book is available from
the British Library. All rights reserved.

Visit our website at www.harpercollins.co.uk

ISBN: 978-0-00-841911-0

Printed and bound in the UK by
Bell & Bain Ltd.

9 11 13 15 17 19 18 16 14 12 10

D1081328

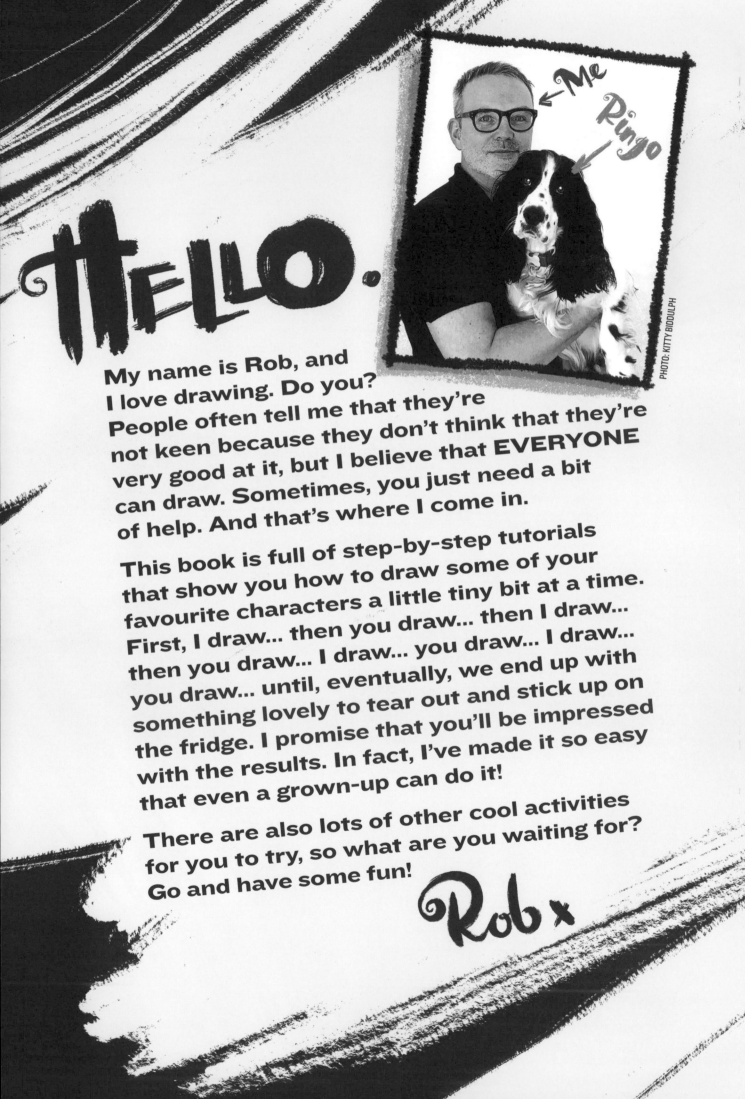

HELLO.

←Me

Ringo

My name is Rob, and I love drawing. Do you? People often tell me that they're not keen because they don't think that they're very good at it, but I believe that EVERYONE can draw. Sometimes, you just need a bit of help. And that's where I come in.

This book is full of step-by-step tutorials that show you how to draw some of your favourite characters a little tiny bit at a time. First, I draw... then you draw... then I draw... then you draw... I draw... you draw... I draw... you draw... until, eventually, we end up with something lovely to tear out and stick up on the fridge. I promise that you'll be impressed with the results. In fact, I've made it so easy that even a grown-up can do it!

There are also lots of other cool activities for you to try, so what are you waiting for? Go and have some fun!

Rob x

You will need...

A pencil...

or a pen...

MANGAKA FLEXIBLE
Kuretake

A pencil sharpener...

An eraser...

GREGOSAURUS
ERASER

and something to colour with.

CRAYON

CRAYON

CRAYON

CRAYON

CRAYON

CRAYON

CRAYON

CRAYON

CRAYON

CRAYON

Okay,
let's get started!

Boo

Meet the DINOSA

Ziggy

Nancy

Winnie

Hector

Martin l'Oeuf

UR JUNIORS

Hi. I'm **Greg** and I'm a stegosaurus. And guess what!? You can learn to draw me and my friend Nancy right here in this book! First, though, my friends need some colour. Can you help?

Otto

Wilf

Sue

How to DRAW...
Gregosaurus

From the book *Dinosaur Juniors: Happy Hatchday*

1 First, draw a very simple **U** shape at the bottom of your page, slightly right of centre.

2 Next, from the top left of your **U** shape, draw a curved line out and upwards.

3 Make a sharp left before heading up again, then curve around to the right and head back over the top.

4 Then head back towards where you started. Before you get there go right for a small uphill detour. Then make a u-turn and head home.

5 Draw in another **U** shape at the bottom, to the left. Now he has legs! Add two more, as shown, for Greg's hands. Don't forget his claws.

6 In the middle of his head, draw a big circle with a dot in the middle. Add a line for an eyebrow, a curve for a smile and a swirl for his nostril. Hello, Greg!

7 Now add his back plates. Start with a big diamond shape on top of his head, with three lines in it. Draw six more all the way down his back, getting smaller as you go.

8 Draw four small spikes on Greg's tail. Add in small circles and dots along his back, below the back plates, to give his skin a nice texture.

9 And it's time to colour in! My Gregosaurus is green and orange, but nobody really knows what colour dinosaurs were so use whatever colours you like.

GREGOSAURUS

By.. **Age**..........

A day in the life of OTTO & WINNIE

RRRRRIINNG!

Wake up

Breakfast

Long bike ride

DINO KRISPLES

ORANGE CRUSH

Run outside

Frisbee

Football

15 things to find in this picture

1 Three fried eggs ☐
2 A running race ☐
3 A saxophone ☐
4 Four dino-sheep ☐
5 A flying saucer ☐
6 Some crayons ☐
7 A dandelion ☐
8 A unicycle ☐
9 A yellow toad ☐
10 A flask ☐
11 Two hula-hoops ☐
12 A pizza ☐
13 An alarm clock ☐
14 An alien ☐
15 Four tortoises ☐

HOW to DRAW...

Nancy

From the book *Dinosaur Juniors: Give Peas a Chance*

GIVE PEAS a Chance

1 Time to draw Nancy the spinosaurus. We're going to start with something easy: a simple U shape.

2 Then add a curved line coming from the top left part of the U.

3 Next, draw a long, curvy shape like this. This will be Nancy's head.

4 Then head back to where we started, but veer off to the right before you get there. This is her tail.

5 Next, add another leg, two arms and some claws.

6 Time to wake Nancy up. Draw a circle with a dot in the middle of it. Then add three eyelashes.

7 Let's give Nancy a lovely big grin. Follow the shape of the eye when you are drawing your curve. Add a little line for an eyebrow too.

8 Time to add her spine. The vertical line should line up with the vertical line of her tummy.

9 Now colour Nancy in. She can be any colour you want. Maybe you could add stripes or patterns?

By.. Age ....

DRAW WITH ROB

NANCY

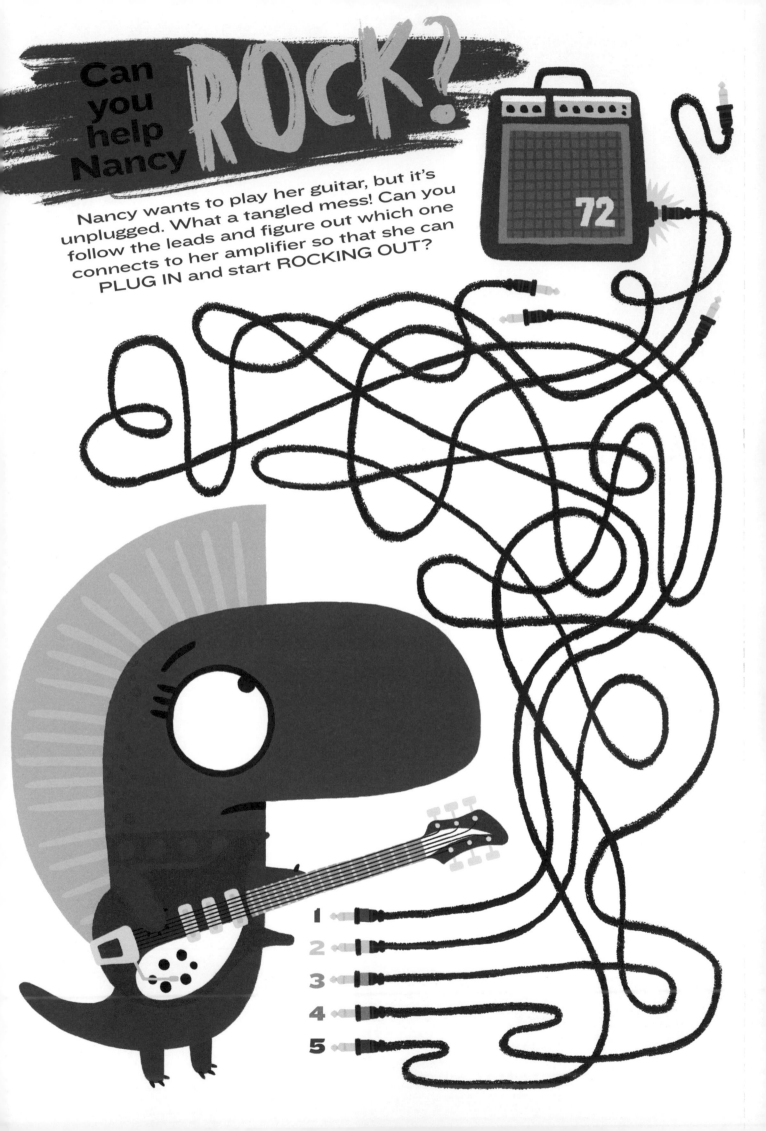

Can you help Nancy ROCK?

Nancy wants to play her guitar, but it's unplugged. What a tangled mess! Can you follow the leads and figure out which one connects to her amplifier so that she can PLUG IN and start ROCKING OUT?

72

1
2
3
4
5

PENGUIN BLUE

Meet

This is Penguin Blue. He lives in Antarctica with his friends, like Clive the polar bear.* You can read all about them in **Blown Away**, but first let's learn how to draw Blue...

* Polar bears don't usually live in Antarctica. They live in the Arctic. But Clive here went fishing one day and got blown off course!

HOW to DRAW...
Penguin Blue

From the books *Blown Away* and *Sunk!*

1 Let's start by drawing a rectangle with rounded corners, right in the middle of the page.

2 Then add a **V** about a third of the way down the rectangle, in the middle. That's Blue's beak.

3 From the top right of the **V**, draw a smaller rectangle inside your bigger rectangle. Follow it around until you reach the other side of the **V**, and join them up.

4 Now let's add two semi-circles at the edges of the rectangle, towards the top. One on each side.

5 Inside the semi-circles, draw a small circle with a dot in the middle. Penguin Blue is now awake!

6 Between Blue's eyes and above his beak, draw two rectangular shapes, as shown.

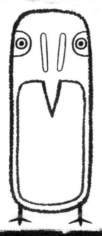

7 Legs and feet next. They're super easy! Just draw two straight lines down from the bottom of Blue's body and then add two smaller lines either side of each one.

8 For the wings, draw a line on each side of Blue's body that curves down and gently outwards.

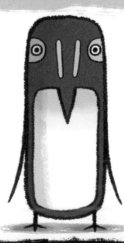

9 Once you've added a scribbly shadow under Penguin Blue's feet, it's time to colour him in. Use any colours you like.

PENGUIN BLUE

BUTTERFLY HUNT

Penguin Blue and the gang have landed in the jungle after a long kite flight. Can you find **ten butterflies** hidden somewhere on these pages – as well as a new friend waiting to play with them?

Hats Off!

Penguin Blue and the gang love to play dress-up, and their costume of choice is... **PIRATES**! Blue here looks fab, but the rest of the crew are missing their hats. Can you help them out?

Penguin Jeff

Penguin Flo

Wilbur Seal

Pirate Parrot

Captain Walker Plank

Clive

SPOT the DIFFERENCE

A very windy day

It's a bit blustery here in the Antarctic. See if you can spot the **six** differences between these two stormy scenes and write what they are in the spaces below.

1

2

3

4

5

6

Meet TEDDY

How do you do? I'm Edward Pugglesworth, but you can call me Teddy. You can read all about me and my human Dave in **Dog Gone** (watch out for the TERRIBLE TROLL!), but for now Mr Biddulph will show you how to draw... ME! Aren't you lucky?

Teddy AKA Edward Pugglesworth

From the book *Dog Gone*

DOG GONE
THE DAY I LOST MY HUMAN
Rob Biddulph

1 Let's start by drawing a thin rectangle across the middle of the page, with a line of tiny circles inside it.

2 Then draw a big curved dome on top.

3 Next, add two triangles, one on each side, for ears, like you see here.

4 Draw two small circles level with the bottom of the ears, one on each side. And then a circle in the space between them, but don't join it up – leave a gap, as shown.

5 In each small circle, draw another circle with a dot in it. These are Teddy's eyes. Above those, add two small baked-bean shapes for eyebrows.

6 Next, add the detail, as shown. He needs a tuft of hair, some lines on his forehead, a mouth with a tooth sticking up, a nose (with tiny spirals for nostrils), and some dots for whiskers.

7 Tricky bit this: draw a curved line down from the right side of his collar, tracing the shape of his front foot, as shown. Do the same on the left side with his back foot. Then join his belly in the middle.

8 Add a little spiral to his bottom for a tail, and give Teddy's collar a tag with his name on it. Also, add his front left and his back left legs.

9 Finally, it's time to colour in your Teddy! I've used normal pug colours, but what will yours look like?

By.. Age..............

What's in THE SHED?

What have Teddy and Dave spotted in the spooky shed? Could it possibly be the **TERRIBLE TROLL** that they've heard so much about? Why don't you draw what you think is hiding in there?

Dog-Spotting

Woof! Can you spot all the different breeds of dog named below? Once you've found them, why don't you give them all names?

- [ ] Cocker Spaniel
- [ ] Labrador
- [ ] Airedale Terrier
- [ ] Pomeranian x2
- [ ] Yorkshire Terrier
- [ ] Corgi
- [ ] Dachshund
- [ ] Rough Collie
- [ ] Alsatian
- [ ] Rottweiler
- [ ] Chihuahua
- [ ] Jack Russell
- [ ] Schnauzer
- [ ] Golden Retriever
- [ ] Bedlington Terrier
- [ ] Dalmatian
- [ ] Poodle
- [ ] French Bulldog
- [ ] Border Terrier

Meet FRED BEAR and EUGENE the OWL

GYM 72

When Fred lost his GRRRRR! just before the Best Bear in the Wood contest, Eugene helped him find it. Since then they've been the best of friends. Why don't I show you how to draw them?

From the book *GRRRRR!*

1 Let's start by drawing a small rectangle almost at the very top of the page. This is Fred's headband. Give it some stripes.

2 Add two semi-circles on top, at each end of the headband, and put two smaller semi-circles inside them. These are Fred's ears.

3 Draw a big curved line down from the headband, like a long, shaggy **U** shape, as shown.

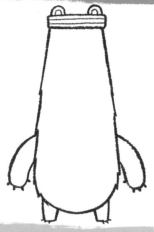

4 For Fred's arms, draw a long sausage shape on each side, as I have here. Add two square shapes at the bottom for his legs. Now add some tiny lines for claws.

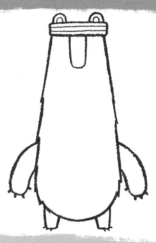

5 Draw a long sausage shape down from the middle of Fred's headband. This drawing features quite a lot of sausage shapes, doesn't it?

6 Next, add two dots for his eyes. At the bottom of the sausage shape, add another little sausage. This time colour it black. Join it to the bottom edge with a small line. Under that, add two semi-circles.

7 Now we need to give Fred a medal. Draw a circle in the middle of his tummy (I've put a paw print in mine) and add a little chimney shape on top of it.

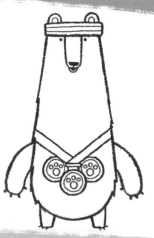

8 From the top of the chimney shape, draw two diagonal lines heading upwards on each side. These are the ribbons to hold his medals. You can add more medals if you like. My Fred has three.

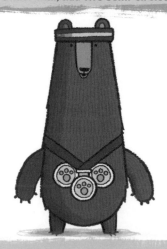

9 Finally, give your bear some colour. Mine is brown with purple and gold accessories. What a winner!

FRED BEAR

By... Age...............

Best Bea

READY, TEDDY, GO!

Today's the day the bears compete to be named Best Bear in the Wood! But who's ready to race, and who will win? Use the spaces to draw and colour in the different bears in the line-up, and don't forget to give your winner a gold medal.

1   2   3

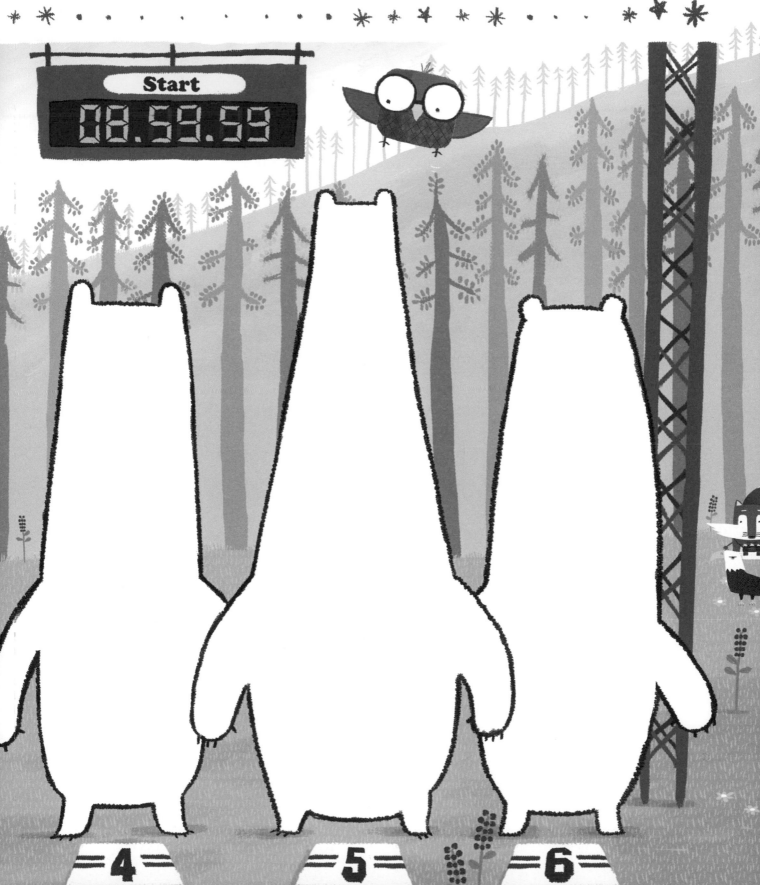

Eugene the owl

From the book *GRRRRR!*

1 Start by drawing two big circles in the middle of the page. Leave a small gap between them.

2 Put a big dot in the middle of each circle, then join them together with a small, horizontal line.

3 Under that line, add a V for Eugene's beak, as I have done here.

4 Now for the body. Put your circles inside a square shape with rounded corners.

5 Draw two short lines down from the bottom corners of your rounded square shape. Add two more little lines at the bottom of each. Look! Eugene has claws!

6 Give him a little tuft of feathers by drawing some scribbly lines coming out of the top of his head.

7 For his wings, draw a line down from the bottom of his left eye, directly below the pupil, and curve it over to Eugene's side. Do that on his right side too.

8 Eugene needs some more feathers. You can add these by filling in the spaces shown with tiny lines.

9 Your Eugene is almost ready to fly! Fill him with colour; you can even give him a pattern on his belly like I have here.

EUGENE the OWL

By .... Age ....

Here in glamorous Doggywood, every day is a chance to be the brightest and most colourful you can be. No one knows that better than this **Odd Dog**, but her friends need some help. Can you colour them in and brighten their day?

A sausage dog

From the book
Odd Dog Out

1 Let's start with a simple rectangle, but with rounded corners. Draw it at a slight angle like this.

2 Next, add two small circles at the top of the rectangle. Put a small black dot in the middle of each one.

3 Time to draw the nose. It's a black rectangle with two swirly bits sticking out of it, and some tiny dots for whiskers.

4 Next, it's the ears. A sausage dog's ears are the same length as its head.

5 Now draw two vertical lines with some arms at the bottom of them.

6 Continue the lines down towards the bottom of your page, and join them up in a curve.

7 Add some little feet and a waggly tail. If you draw two tiny lines either side of the tail it makes it look like it's moving.

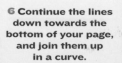

8 Now, the fun part! Dress your sausage dog in any outfit you like. Mine is dressed as a hot dog. Turn the page for lots more examples of doggy costumes.

SAUSAGE DOG

By.. Age...........

Doggy DRESS-UP

All Odd Dogs love to dress up and stand out! Can you come up with some colourful costumes for these three?

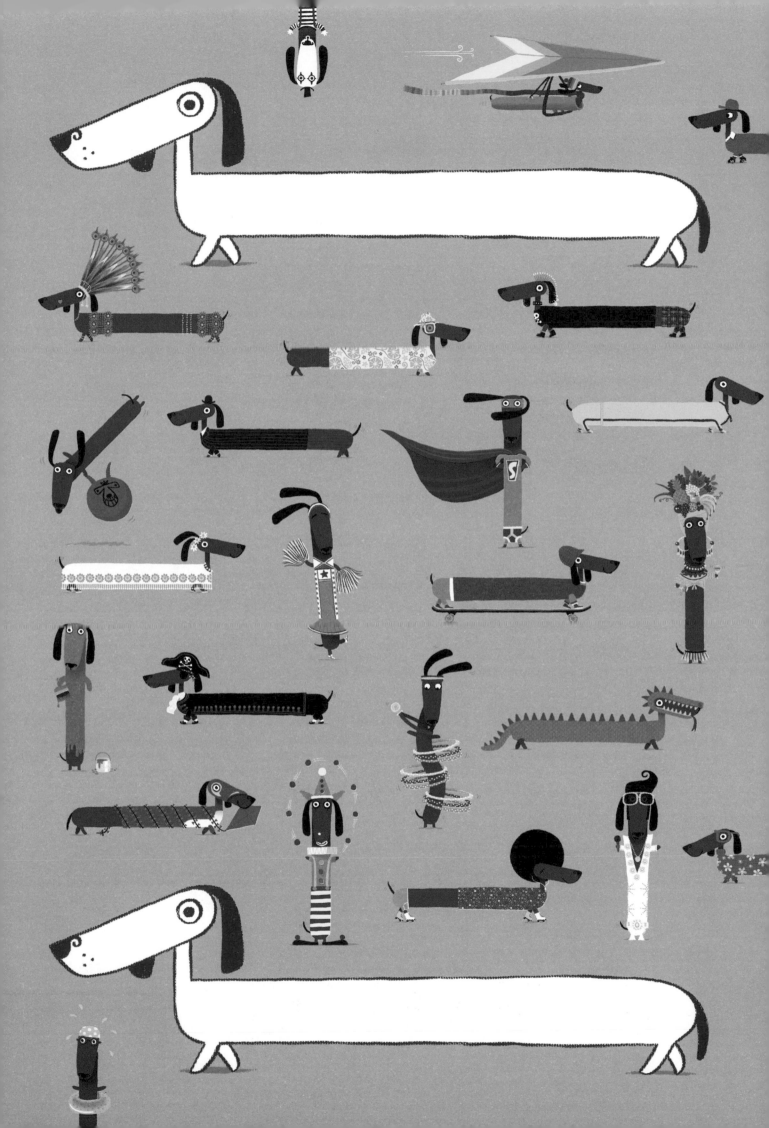

HUNT the HOT DOG

Somewhere among these dressed-up dogs is a real hot dog in a bun! Can you find it?

Zorg the Explorer has come all the way from Alpha Centauri so you can learn how to draw him. Let's get started before he flies away!

COFFEE

Meet

ZORG

the EXPLORER

How to Draw... Zorg the Explorer

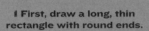

1 First, draw a long, thin rectangle with round ends.

2 Next, add two vertical lines coming out of each end of the rectangle.

3 Now draw a big circle right in the middle of your two vertical lines.

4 Inside that circle, draw a slightly smaller circle.

5 Inside that circle draw an even smaller circle and colour it in. Leave two even tiner circles white inside that circle. Add eyelashes.

6 Next, join up the two vertical lines with a big curve.

7 Let's make our alien smile. Draw a big curvy grin and add two small lines, one at each end.

8 Next, add a few freckles on each cheek and two pointy fangs coming down from each end of the mouth.

9 Now for our alien's antennae. Each one is made up of two vertical lines with an egg shape sitting on top of them.

10 Now the tricky bit. Draw in some lovely, wiggly tentacles, like this.

11 Then add lots of little semi-circle suckers.

12 Finally, colour your alien in. Use any colours you like. There are no rules. Have fun!

ZORG the EXPLORER

By.. Age............

SHOW & TELL

It's the most exciting day of the week!
Class 2L always bring in the BEST things for
Show and Tell day. Use your drawing
skills to show us what they are!

What kind of creature is **Eddie** holding?

Can you decorate **Kenzo**'s balloon?

What has **Jessie** got in her bottle?

What on earth is
Parmida balancing on
her head?

Holly has brought in
a fantastic robot. But what
does he look like?

with Class 2L

What famous work of art has **Isaac** brought in to show us?

What is in **Florence**'s fish tank?

Nelly has brought in Susan, her pet dragon. Can you show us what she looks like?

What kind of amazing food does **George** have on his plate?

What's that coming out of **Lily**'s lamp?

The GREAT ALiEN BOTTOM-SWAP

Aliens come in all shapes and sizes. **Zorg the Explorer** has tentacles, but swap in any bottom you like for his friends. Do they have wheels? Or rocket jets? Maybe they run around on chicken legs? Anything goes, so fire up that imagination and get drawing!

Meet **Kevin**

And this is **SID**

Kevin and **Sid** are best friends, even if Kevin is imaginary. They make the world a more magical place by really believing in each other. Let's make your world more magical too, by learning to draw Kevin.

HOW to DRAW...
Kevin

From the book *Kevin*

1 Let's start with a big circle, right in the middle of your page. If you give it some shaggy edges it will look like your Kevin is furry.

2 Give Kevin a big smile by drawing a curved line inside the circle, along the bottom.

3 At each end of the smile, draw two small circles with dots in them. Voilà! Kevin is awake!

4 Let's make Kevin extra smiley by adding in some eyebrows. Draw two tilted lines above his eyes, as above. Also, give him a little tuft of fur on top of his head!

5 Give Kevin one big tooth by drawing half a square with curved edges towards the right-hand side of his mouth.

6 Time to give Kevin a body! Draw a smaller circle underneath his big round head.

7 Add two big sausage shapes for his arms, with two stubby rectangles underneath for his legs.

8 Let's give Kevin some lovely spots! Add them around his eye, on the top of his head, all over his arms and legs... wherever you like!

9 Finally, give him some scribbly shadow by his feet and colour him in. My Kevin is vanilla and pink – what colour is yours?

KEVIN

By.. Age.............

Sid's IMAGINARY WORLD

Sid has come to visit Kevin in his magical land of make-believe... but this wonderful world isn't so bright without its colour! Let your imagination run wild and give it back its magic.

Slimy

Frilly

Leggy

The one shaped like a kidney

Big
Red

Kevin

Little
Blue

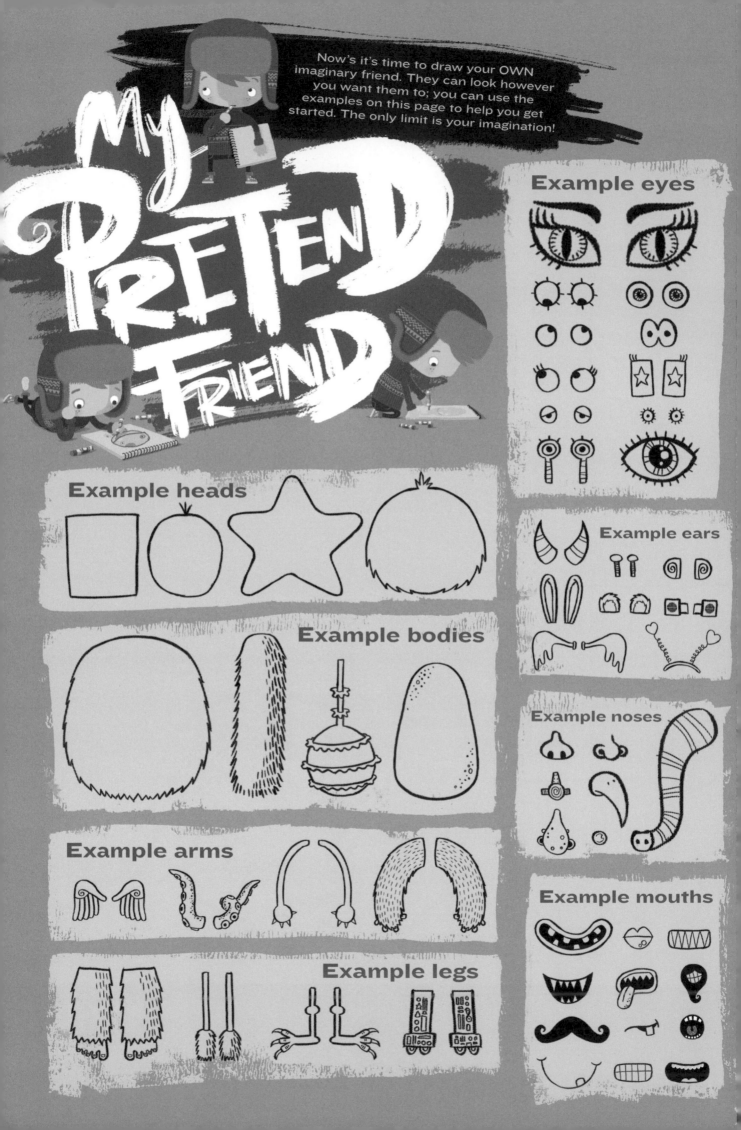

MY PRETEND FRIEND

Now's it's time to draw your OWN imaginary friend. They can look however you want them to; you can use the examples on this page to help you get started. The only limit is your imagination!

Example eyes

Example heads

Example bodies

Example ears

Example noses

Example arms

Example mouths

Example legs

My pretend friend is called...

kevin

Wow – your drawing is amazing! And you've
become an awesome artist, just like Sid. Turn the page
for your award from me and the rest of the gang...

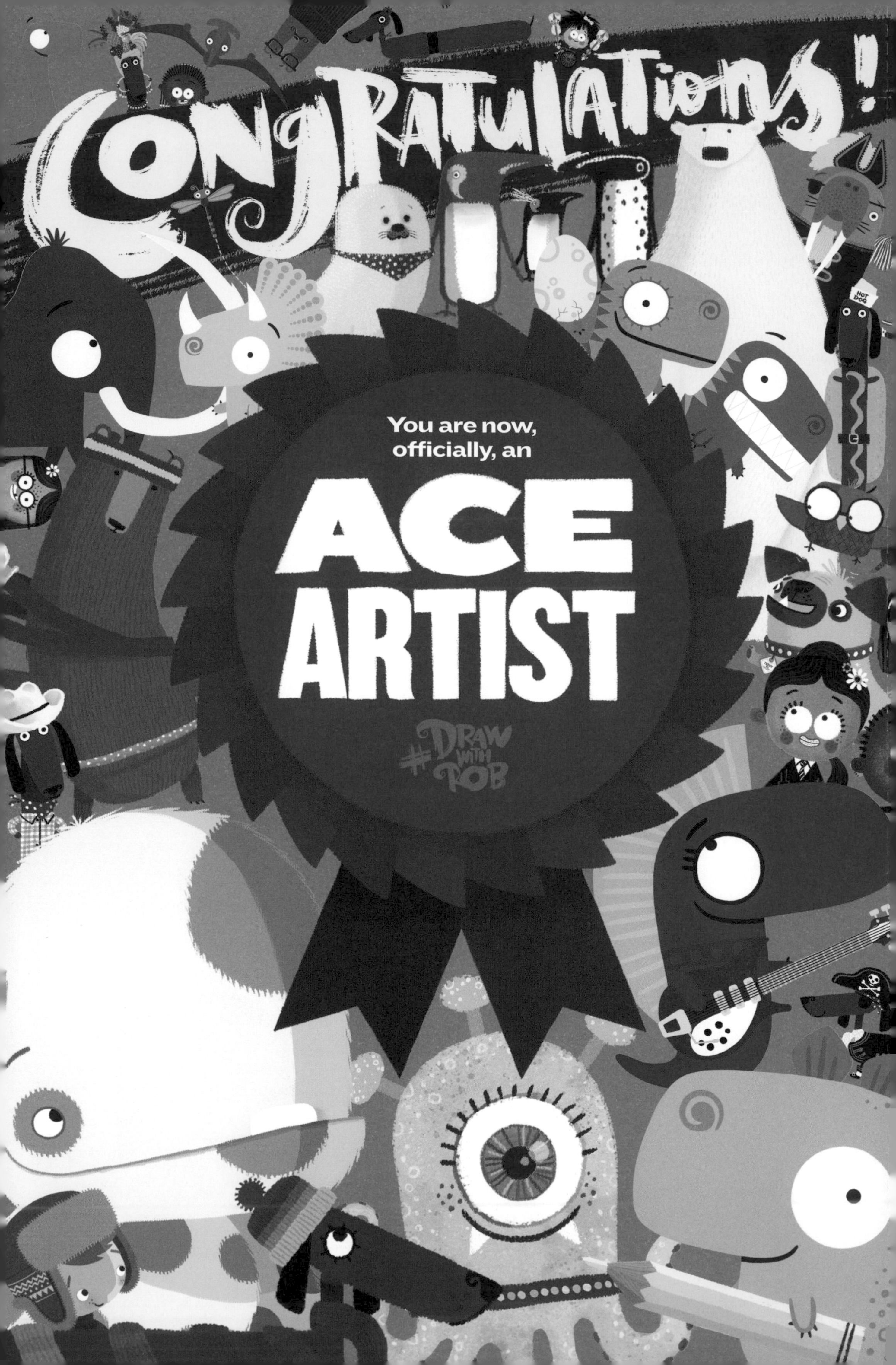

CONGRATULATIONS!

You are now,
officially, an

ACE
ARTIST

#Draw
with
ROB

This is to certify that

is officially an

ACE ARTIST

WHO CAN DRAW DINOSAURS, PENGUINS, PUGS, BEARS, OWLS, SAUSAGE DOGS DRESSED AS HOT DOGS, ALIENS AND IMAGINARY FRIENDS

Rob Biddulph

President of drawing stuff

Date

Back of certificate

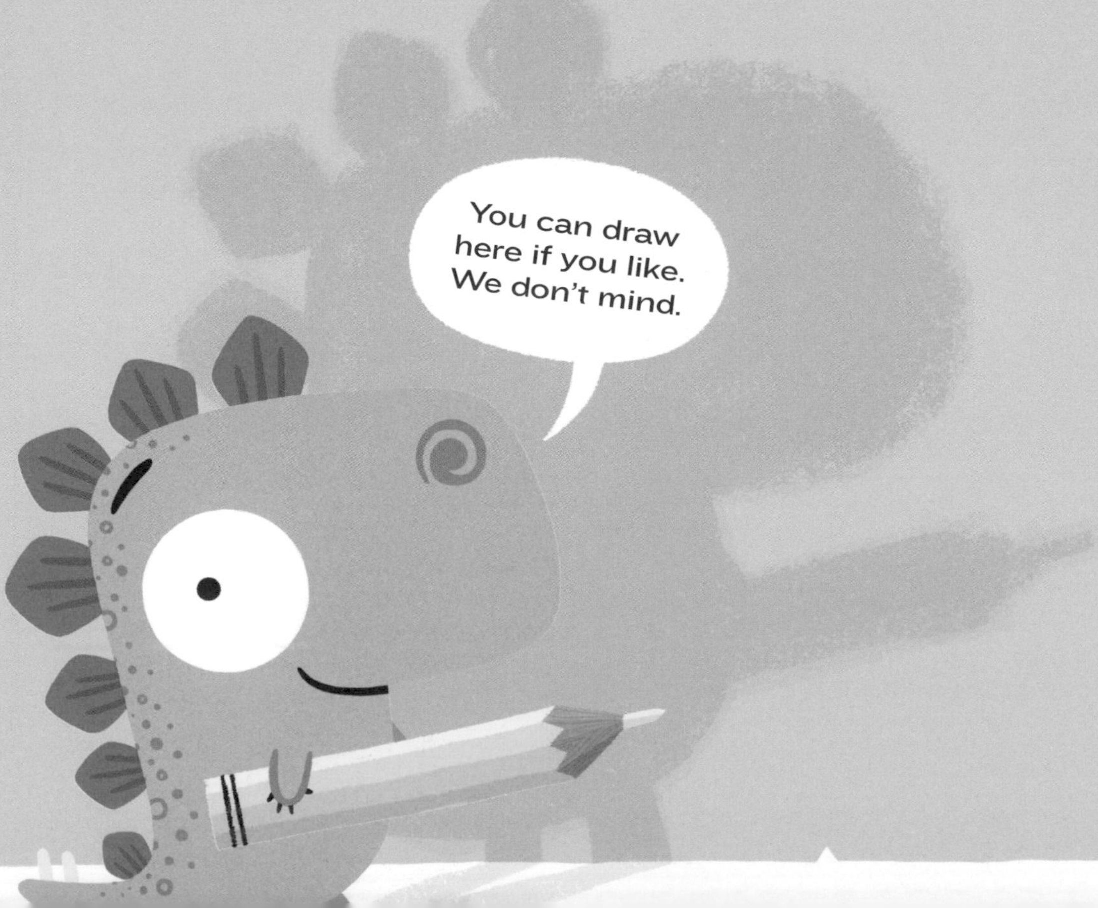

ALL ABOUT ME

Before we start, take a good look at yourself in the mirror. Looking really closely at whatever it is that you're drawing is one of the most important parts of being an artist. These pages will help you think about not only what you look like but who you are.

My eyes

Blue ☐

Green ☐

Brown ☐

Grey ☐

Pink with yellow spots ☐

Rainbow ☐

Stuff I like

My favourite **colour** is ....

My favourite **food** is ....

My favourite **song** is ....

My favourite **movie** is ....

My favourite **sport** is ....

My favourite **toy** is ....

My favourite **book** is ....

My favourite **author** is ....

My favourite **animal** is ....

My favourite **thing to do** is ....

My hairstyle

Add your own

My hair colour

Add your own

Clothes, etc.

A self-portrait

1 Start with a big circle right in the middle of your page. This is your head. If your head is more like a square, a heart, a rectangle or an oval, draw that instead!

2 Let's add your eyes. Add two circles towards the bottom of your head.

3 Add two dots in the middle of these circles. In between the eyes draw a short vertical line with a bump at the bottom. This is your nose.

4 Give yourself some lovely eyebrows and eyelashes, like I have here, by adding some little lines. Add a small curved line for a smile, and there you are.

5 Next, add a semi-circle on either side of your head for your ears. Don't forget the swirly line inside for the middle bit.

6 Let's add your body next. You can add a square shape, like I have here, but make it bigger or smaller or longer or shorter to make it look more like you.

7 Add two diagonal rectangles for arms. Draw a semi-circle at the end of each with five little semi-circles coming out of it, and there are your hands!

8 Give yourself some legs by drawing two vertical rectangles coming down from your body. Add a couple of horizontal rectangles at the bottom for feet.

9 And it's finally time to make your portrait look like YOU! Draw your hair, add in your clothes and any extra bits. Wow! There you are. Don't forget to sign your portrait.

SELF-PORTRAIT

By.. Age............

GOODBYE!

Well done for reaching the end of this book. I really hope that you've enjoyed drawing with me. Now, why not get to know the characters that you've drawn by reading their stories in my books?

And don't forget to watch all of my **#DrawWithRob** videos on my YouTube channel and follow me on social media

ANSWERS

A DAY IN THE LIFE OF OTTO & WINNIE

BUTTERFLY HUNT

SPOT THE DIFFERENCE

HUNT THE HOT DOG

CAN YOU HELP NANCY ROCK?

Lead 3 leads to the amplifier.

DOG-SPOTTING

1 Airedale Terrier
2 Alsatian
3 Rottweiler
4 Schnauzer
5 Cocker Spaniel
6 Corgi
7 Dalmatian
8 Golden Retriever
9 Yorkshire Terrier
10 Pomeranians x2
11 Chihuahua
12 Jack Russell
13 Bedlington Terrier
14 Poodle
15 Rough Collie
16 French Bulldog
17 Labrador
18 Border Terrier
19 Daschund

72